Les Points de Seurat/Seurat's Dots

Learn Shapes in French and English

OUI LOVE BOOKS

ODÉON LIVRE

CHICAGO MMXIX

Featuring Georges Seurat's "Un dimanche après-midi à l'Île de la Grande Jatte"

by Ethan Safron
French Books Chicago, LLC

Edited by Joseph Feinberg

A read-aloud version of this title is available online. To access this video, you may scan the QR code below or type `ouilovebooks.com/seurat-audio` into your web browser.

ouilovebooks.com/seurat-audio

DOT

·

LE POINT

CIRCLE

LE CERCLE

OVAL

L'OVALE

TRIANGLE

LE TRIANGLE

SQUARE

LE CARRÉ

RECTANGLE

LE RECTANGLE

L'ARC

SPIRAL

LA SPIRALE

Let's Review!

Révisons !

LE CARRÉ

LE TRIANGLE

OVAL

CIRCLE

L'OVALE

LE CERCLE

CIRCLE

OVAL

TRIANGLE

LE CERCLE

L'OVALE

LE   TRIANGLE

FIN